Fifty Things I Love About My Wife

LOVE IS THE ONLY WAY

Dedicated to my wonderful Wife

"Ishpreet Jha"

"Love is a symbol of eternity. It wipes out all sense of time, destroying all memory of a beginning and all fear of an end"

-- Quote by Madame de Stael

COPYRIGHT

Printed by Maxlife Publishing

Edited by Judith Rooney
Cover Design by Keshav Jha

Printed in Australia
First Printing Edition, 2021
Ebook - ISBN 978-1-922580-00-9

Printed: ISBN 978-1-922580-01-6

A catalogue record for this book is available from the National Library of Australia

www.MaxLifePublishing.com

"This book exemplifies the principles of love, trust and gratitude toward one's partner."
FOREWORD BY DR. JOHN DEMARTINI
World-renowned Human Behaviour Specialist who featured in the international documentary movie - 'The Secret'

FIFTY THINGS I LOVE
ABOUT MY WIFE
LOVE IS THE ONLY WAY

Includes

16 Principles of Love for Better Relationships

"This book humbles me and makes me look deeply again into my own relationships. Thank you for the inspiration of your life and work."
- WIM HOF, also known as 'The Iceman'

KESHAV JHA

AUTHOR - KESHAV JHA

FOREWORD BY – DR. JOHN DEMARTINI

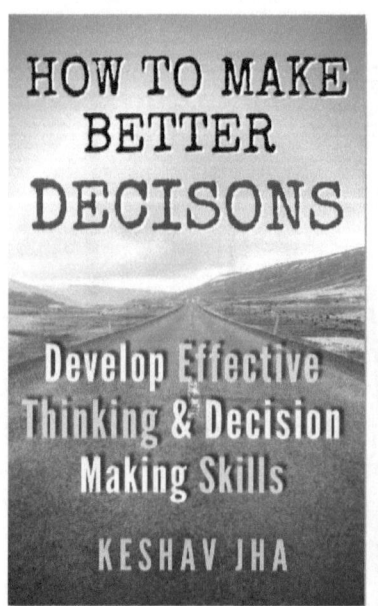

HOW TO MAKE BETTER DECISONS

Develop Effective Thinking & Decision Making Skills

KESHAV JHA

BEING

Become Happy in as Little as 30 Seconds NOW

HAPPY

200

PROVEN EASY & QUICK WAYS TO BECOME MORE HAPPY

KESHAV JHA

Upcoming Books – Visit www.MaxlifePublishing.com

SURESHOT WAYS TO ACHIEVE GOALS

3 Steps Goal Setting For Teenageers

KESHAV JHA

POWERFUL & EFFECTIVE "Me Time" STRATEGIES

HOW TO FILL YOUR OWN CUP

200 SELF-LOVE IDEAS "Learn to Love Yourself"

KESHAV JHA

STOP PROCRASTINATION 100 SMART STRATEGIES FOR OVERCOMING PROCRASTINATION

KESHAV JHA

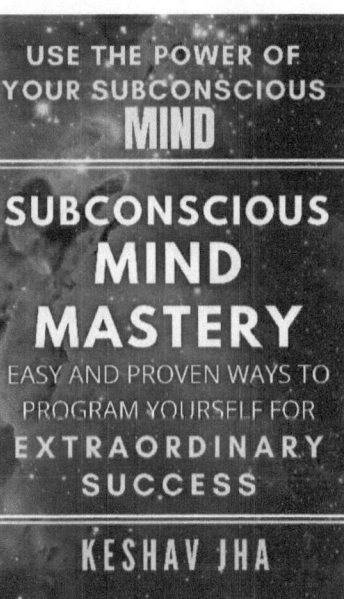

USE THE POWER OF YOUR SUBCONSCIOUS MIND

SUBCONSCIOUS MIND MASTERY EASY AND PROVEN WAYS TO PROGRAM YOURSELF FOR EXTRAORDINARY SUCCESS

KESHAV JHA

Upcoming Books – Visit www.MaxlifePublishing.com

ANCIENT WISDOM for ENGLIGHTENED LIVING YOGA VASHISHTA Simplified

KESHAV JHA

YOGA For BETTER LIVING CREATE HIGH ENERGY LIFE! DEVELOP HEALTHY MIND AND BODY

KESHAV JHA

Free App Offer within the Book for Developing Positive Mindset

This affirmation app has inbuilt brainwaves sound and white noise which can be used for developing positive mindset. This app can help you to stay focused on your core desirable values and achieve your goals. The brainwaves synchronization has been found to enhance relaxation response and positive influence cognitive abilities. There are six categories of affirmations included - happiness, health, success, wealth, relationship, and weight loss. Each of these categories have 15 affirmations which can be further edited to give it more personal touch for improved effectiveness. You can even add more categories and affirmations or edit or delete the existing ones to have unique user experience and customization.

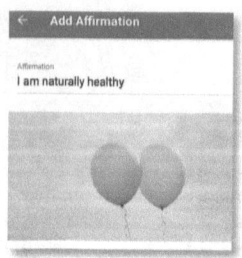

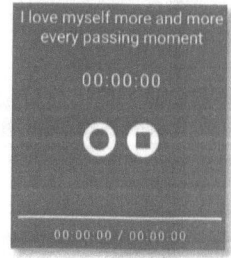

This App is compatible ONLY with Android smartphones and tablets
This App is NOT COMPATIBLE with iOS (Apple) smartphones and tablets

PRAISE FOR THE BOOK

"Fifty Things I Love About My Wife: Love is the Only Way is a beautiful and graceful reminder to everyone who wants to proactively enrich their relationship; to give it greater meaning, and make it deeper and more rewarding."

Houston, Texas, United States
-- Dr John Demartini, world-renowned Human Behaviour Specialist, researcher, global educator and international best-selling author of "The Values Factor", who featured in "The Secret", a documentary film released in 2006, which transformed millions of lives

"Fifty Things I Love About My Wife is a wonderful book, celebrating what it means to love someone unconditionally. Keshav lovingly shows how it is possible to be grateful for the small everyday things our partners do, as well as the big things, and that by focusing on making our relationships stronger, we can have long and successful relationships. The list of 'Things' Keshav loves about his wife is heartwarming, while the final chapters offer real practical advice for how to have a long and successful relationship."

London, England, United Kingdom
-- Stephanie Brown, Property Investor, Career Coach, Keynote Speaker, previously Marketing Manager at Apple and Nike and author of life-transforming book - "Fired: Why Losing Your Job Is the Best Thing That Can Happen to You"

"Family is everything. Finding the right partner in life with whom to create a family is so important. I am so pleased that Keshav found Ishpreet and together they have built a life of love and happiness. If this book can help spread and reinforce family values for one person, our world will be a better place."

Springfield, Queensland, Australia
-- Maha Sinnathamby, Founder & Visionary - Greater Springfield. World's Best Master Planned Community 2010, Philanthropist, Recipient - Ernst and Young Master Entrepreneur of the Year Award and inspiration behind the book - "Stop Not Till the Goal is Reached: The 10 Principles for Fearless Success"

"What a beautiful and heartfelt expression of love! After 20-plus years of marriage many people are hitting massive bumps in the road; this is a testament to what can happen when you "choose love" every day. Keshav has shared some practical strategies that have enhanced his 27-year relationship on how to reconnect with your spouse, grow together and strengthen your relationship."

Burleigh, Queensland, Australia
-- Sarah Megginson, Senior Editor, Journalist & Writer - Home Loans, Cosmopolitan, Marie Claire, Your Investment Property and author of business book - "How To Make Money By Working From Home: The step-by-step guide to successful freelancing"

"How refreshing to read of one man's enduring love for his wife! Keshav Jha honours his wife beautifully and offers time-proven, intimately developed, basic and simple principles for rejuvenating and growing any marriage relationship. Essential reading for all who wish to create a lasting family legacy."

Addison, Texas, United States
-- Tom Ziglar, CEO, Ziglar, Inc., proud son of Zig Ziglar and author of the inspiring and motivational book - "Choose to Win: Transform Your Life, One Simple Choice at a Time"

"What an amazing tribute to Keshav's wife and true family values! In an easy-to-read format, this book reveals so many levels and facets of love and gratitude that have a powerful impact on the reader. It's humbling to witness this expression of true love. Readers could find great benefit from applying the 16 principles of love which have sustained their togetherness, creating a long lasting and fulfilling relationship".

Maitland, NSW, Australia
-- Roseanne Gaut, Owner - Dowling Real Estate, Maitland NSW, Recipient - Property Manager of the Year 2012 Award sponsored by "Your Investment Property", Australia

"Reading your book humbles me and makes me look again deeply into my own relationships. More men and women should ask these questions! Devotion to our partner is the blue of the sky, from which clouds of confusion dissipate. Endorsing this book is a pleasure, as it reminds me of accepting my own responsibility for making sure relationships reflect higher love. Therefore, I thank you for your work and life as an inspiration to all who love, and wish to be loved in return."

Amsterdam, North Holland, Netherlands
-- Wim Hof, also known as 'The Iceman', holder of 21 Guinness World Records for extraordinary feats of human endurance and author of the New York Times bestseller - "The Wim Hof Method"

"This book is the most unique gift Keshav could have given to Ishpreet. It outlines the true value of love and the importance of their family values. A true romance story with lots of love and emotional experiences that show how to a build a strong relationship."

Melbourne, Victoria, Australia
-- Vanessa De Sensi, Senior Property Manager and Licensed Estate Agent - Barry Plant Craigieburn

"Fifty Things I Love About My Wife, is an insightful and meaningful journey of the long-standing relationship between Keshav and Ishpreet. The guiding principles are useful in so many aspects of our everyday lives, but most importantly, how to love and respect our life partners in a way that is appreciated by them. This easy-to-read book, with many personal photographs, guides the reader both through their relationship, and the process of reconnecting, and maintaining our own relationships".

Adelaide, SA, Australia
-- Deborah Daken, Senior Property Manager - Turner Real Estate, Recipient - Real Estate Institute Awards for Excellence - Large Property Management Agency

"The world probably doesn't need more billionaires, but desperately needs more loving & compassionate humans like Keshav. And love, compassion & caring starts from our homes. Keshav's love and care for his better half reflect a narrative similar to that of my intellectual companion in all my books - that of a truly 'better' half."

New Delhi, India
-- Manoj Arora, Gold Medalist - AMU, Aligarh India, previously worked at L&T, TCS and IBM and best-selling author of - "A Father's Diary", "Happiness Unlimited", "Dream On", "From the Rat Race to Financial Freedom" & "Autobiography of a Stock"

"What an amazing read and such a timely reminder of how to be gracious and demonstrate and acknowledge unconditional love. Keshav, this is a true reflection of what a humble caring person you are and what an amazing family you have with Ishpreet and the girls. I took this read as a timely reminder as to things I could do better in my own relationship. The principles are as simple as they are sound and a great reminder for all couples, relationships and partnerships. This love story is well worth the read and one I will definitely recommend."

Brisbane, QLD, Australia
-- Jacqui Fletcher, Lending Manager - IMB Bank, Previously Branch Manager at Credit Union Australia, St. George Bank and Commonwealth Bank, Recipient - Duke of Edinburg Award

"A fascinating, visually and emotionally inspiring book packed with straightforward easy to follow strategies that can help life partners to elevate their relationship to next level"

Toronto, Ontario, Canada
-- Nishal Nair, HR Business Partner - Humber College, Toronto, Certified Human Resources Leader (CHRL), HR Professionals Association, Canada

"It is a great reminder of how to love and be thankful, and a great guide for young couples in how to cherish love. For me, this was a great book to read, as I recently got married - so thank you and your wife for the wonderful love you shared with everyone and thank you for teaching us that fairytale love is possible when you know the principles of love!"

Prokuplje, Serbia
-- Milena (Aleksić) Milenković, Customer Service - Hotel Hammeum, Prokuplje, previously Cancer Services Executive Support at Liverpool Hospital, NSW, Australia

"What a wonderful gift to provide your partner! To take the time to compose this gift is a reminder to all to stop and reflect on love. I think you are both very lucky to have each other. A practical and definitive book that includes actionable strategies to build loving relationships. I can't wait to see what Keshav does for Ishpreet's 50th Birthday!!"

Sydney, NSW, Australia
-- Tyron Hyde, Director and Owner, Washington Brown, Recipient - NSW State Junior Lawn Bowling Championship and author of best-selling business book - "Keep Claiming It!: A Guide to Property Depreciation"

DEDICATION

Thank you Ishpreet, my beloved wife, for giving me this beautiful card with a real red rose expressing your true and passionate love 25 years ago...

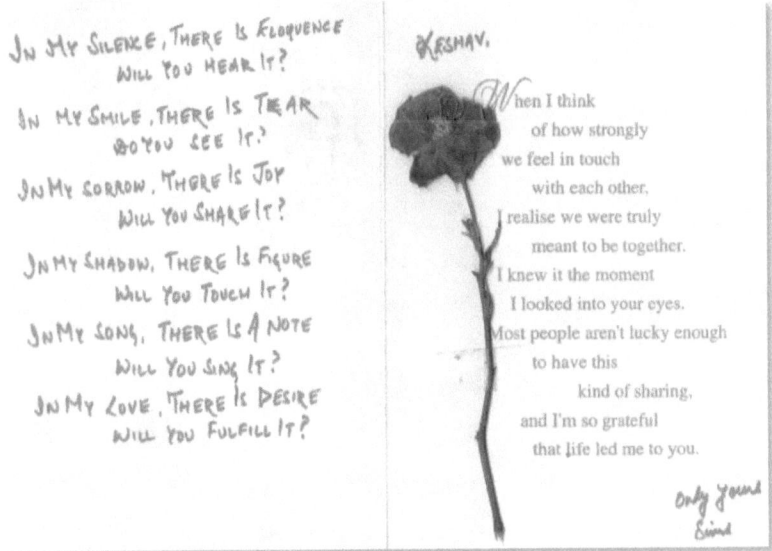

Although the rose has dried yet the message of love it permeates is very much alive in my heart and continues to grow every passing moment. I keep this token of love close to my heart and treasure it very much. I dedicate this book to you and our loving relationship.

CONTENTS

ABOUT THE AUTHOR

 Keshav Jha has worked as a teacher at multiple Australian Colleges and Universities. A teacher, technologist, and researcher by training, Keshav is also a contributing writer to leading Australian business magazines, a business owner and an avid yoga, meditation, and NLP practitioner.

Keshav was fortunate to escape death in Nov 2011 when he drowned in a community swimming pool on a sunny Sunday afternoon, whilst enjoying cool water splashes with his daughter. Luckily, he was rescued by an off-duty police officer attending a family barbeque next to the pool, separated by a fence.

Instant Channel 7 media personality - for two minutes! Thankful for this second chance to live and enjoy seeing his two daughters grow up,

Keshav is committed to living a life of gratitude and is determined to help people live more inspiring, purposeful and productive lives.

Keshav believes that we can all attain inner peace and happiness by concentrating on the universal core values of family, spirituality, respect for others, and honesty in relationships.

Through customised group and one-to-one mentoring programs, he has guided multiple individuals and couples toward achieving their life goals.

By practising his simplified rubric, readers will acquire the skills, knowledge, strategies and tools to become more authentic, passionate, empowered and fulfilled individuals; lovable, dependable and true to self.

Keshav considers that "every picture is worth 1000 words", and writes books with minimal text and more pictorial content in order to maximise learning and engage readers through visual appeal. Less than 10% of people who buy a book read past the first chapter, resulting in the book becoming an aid to "shelf-help" rather than "self-help". Keshav's beautiful illustrations will ensure his book is read completely, and treasured as a keepsake.

He is a passionate learner, researcher and curious person by nature, and holds qualifications in hospitality management, information technology, sustainability, finance and mortgage broking, real-estate and property management. He has received numerous educational, vocational, entrepreneurial and sustainability awards.

He lives in Sydney, Australia with his wife and two daughters.

You can check out Keshav's latest books anytime at MaxlifePublishing.com or visit his website KeshavJha.com.au.

FOREWORD

By Dr John Demartini, Founder of the Demartini Institute

As a human behaviour specialist, professional speaker, author, researcher and business consultant, I am blessed to have the privilege to mentor and coach diverse groups of people across the world; ranging from Wall Street executives, professionals, actors, health care professionals and sports personalities about relationships, wealth, education and business.

I came to know Keshav and his lovely family in 2013 when they attended my live events in Sydney, Australia. Through our interactions, I have come to learn Keshav has a deeply inspired mission and quest for understanding human behaviour and drive to building human relationships.

As human beings, we forge various relationships in our lifetime. However, the most intimate, intricate and the longest of all relationships is one between husband and wife or life partners. As couples, we are driven by a different set of values and as a result face different challenges when trying to live and thrive under the same roof.

Based on global statistics roughly one in two marriages end up in separation which can often be heart wrenching and devasting for either or both partners. When children are involved it can be perceived to be even more traumatic.

Keshav and his partner Ishpreet have a love story that sprawls 27 years. Their love journey is captured in this book in a form of an inspirational memoir where Keshav expresses genuine love and gratitude to the woman in his life, Ishpreet.

Numerous photos are included to encapsulate the tale of their appreciative and affectionate relationship; a heart-warming journey from teenage years to adulthood. The book exemplifies the principles of love, trust and gratitude toward one's partner. How often do we forget to demonstrate or reflect our love and appreciation towards the one special individual we spend most of our lives with?

'Fifty things I love about my wife - Love is the only way' is a beautiful and graceful reminder to everyone who wants to proactively take charge of their relationships; to make it deeper and more meaningful and rewarding. Whichever stage of the relationship you are currently in with your spouse or partner, the 16 principles provided are guaranteed to help you strive and achieve a healthy and loving relationship.

The is an easy to read book but do not be fooled by its simplicity. It truly conveys and articulates the powerful message of love, appreciation and gratitude in a few words with meaningful and complementary pictures. Without too much effort the reader's left and right brain faculties of logic, rationale, emotion and imagination are led to wholistic assimilation of the message of love, thus inspiring action, happily ending in heightened connection and an emotional bond between two.

About Dr. John Demartini

Dr. John Demartini is a world-renowned specialist in human behaviour, a researcher, author and global educator. He has addressed audiences up to 11,000 people at a time across the world and shared the stage with some of the world's most influential people such as Sir Richard Branson, Stephen Covey, Steve Wozniak, Robert Kiyosaki, Tony Fernandes, Wayne Dyer, Deepak Chopra, Donald Trump and many more.

He has been a welcomed guest on Larry King Live, a contributor to Oprah Magazine, and has featured in the international phenomena "The Secret", a documentary film that swept the world in 2006, transforming millions of lives.

Dr. Demartini is the author of over 40 self-development books and manuscripts such as the acclaimed 'The Breakthrough Experience®' which has been translated into over 39 languages. He has produced over 80 CDs and DVDs covering subjects about relationships, finance, education, business, leadership and health. He has worked with entrepreneurs, board members, CEOs, managers, teams and employees for over 48 years in over 100 countries such as India, Iran, USA, SA, UK, Australia, New Zealand, Botswana, Canada, Japan, Singapore and Malaysia, to name a few.

Dr. Demartini has appeared in over 30 documentaries, including The Secret, The Opus,

The Compass and Oh My God, alongside celebrities such as Hugh Jackman, Seal, Ringo Star and Bob Geldof. He has been interviewed by thousands of newspaper and magazine publications, radio and television talk shows across the globe (www.DrDemartini.com/media) and his work has been referenced in over 500 books.

'Your inner most dominant thought determines your outermost tangible reality'

-- Quote by Dr. John Demartini

PREFACE

Dear Ishpreet, thanks for being my life partner. I remember the loneliness that I experienced when I was living alone in Australia and you were in India. Your presence in my life is a pure grace of God. You make my life complete and my existence meaningful. My life feels fulfilled with you.

This photo book encapsulates the last 27 years of our lives together, and is an expression of heartfelt gratitude towards you. The blessed life I have with you and our kids makes me feel very fortunate, content and happy every day.

Hope this book succeeds in expressing how your loving presence has positively impacted my life.

With lots of love, thanks and gratitude...

Yours always...

Keshav

HOW TO USE THIS BOOK

This book is written as a photo book memoir, with minimal text and hundreds of pictures to make it more visual. The author believes that "every picture is worth 1000 words".

Moreover, less than 10% of people who buy any book read past the first chapter, resulting in the book turning into more of "shelf-help" rather than "self-help" situation. The author believes that making the book more visual by using pictures will make it more interesting and engaging, thereby increasing the chances of being read completely rather than partially.

The book has seven chapters in total. The first 4 chapters depict 27 years of the author's relationship with his wife and 50 things that the author likes, appreciates and is thankful to his wife for.

Each chapter is laid out in a visual storytelling style following a progressive timeline, such as when the relationship began, where the author met his wife for the first time, challenges faced by them, marrying and living together after almost

10 years of a long-distance relationship and the arrival of two daughters in their lives, allowing them to experience parenthood together.

The fifth chapter is about the author expressing this gratitude towards the people who have impacted positively on his life and have contributed towards making him a better person.

Chapter six discusses 16 principles of love that have helped the author to create and foster a healthy loving relationship with his wife.

Chapter seven, the final chapter, includes journaling section that can be used by readers to write down their actionable ideas and strategies that are inspired and guided by 16 principles of love which can help readers to make their relationship better, deeper and more fulfilling.

ACKNOWLEDGEMENT

Writing this book has been an internally challenging yet very fulfilling experience.

I must start by thanking my awesome wife, Ishpreet who has been the key source of inspiration for the last 27 years and the reason for this book to be written in the first place.

Writing a book about your life seems surreal. I am forever thankful to my friend Najla Turk for her keen insight and suggestions that have helped immensely in bringing my stories to life.

A very special thanks to my friends Bhim Kharel, Kulwinder Singh, Anuraj Gambhir, Nitin Vaswani and Rohini Seth for enriching our lives through their presence and interactions. Their kind and loving friendship have made a positive difference to the quality of my life.

I am eternally grateful to my late grandfather Bindeshwari Prasad Misra who taught me about the seven core human values essential for a meaningful life - love, passion, courage, dedication, discipline, punctuality and forgiveness.

I am immensely grateful to my father Rabindra Kumar Mishra and my mother Kiran Devi for blessing me with their unconditional love and nurturing from the moment I was born.

A heartfelt thanks to my Uncle Dr. Lakshmishwar Jha for teaching me the importance of good education and for having a curious mind.

I sincerely thank my sister Nina for believing in me and my ability to make a positive difference in this world.

Finally, I thank all the couples out there who aspire to a loving and meaningful relationship with their spouse.

May all those couples succeed in making the best of their lives together and leave a legacy of love, kindness, compassion and, most important of all, forgiveness for the next generation.

CHAPTER ONE

Love at first sight

I fell in love with you the very first time we met each other in 1993 at DAV Public school. I vividly remember the details of our first meeting, knew in my heart that you were special, and felt a unique connection with you instantly which was beyond words and hard to explain. I am thankful to your classmate Dev who encouraged us to meet each other.

When we both met for the first time, you were only 15 years old and I was 17 years old. I did not even know how to correctly spell your name.

Forgive me for initially misspelling your name as "Isprite". Thanks for being with me on this 27-year special journey called life, which has been wonderful.

Thank you for waving at me at DAV school in 1993 which lead to the beginning of our loving relationship that has resulted in two beautiful kids and lots of good memories to cherish for the rest of our lives...

2nd

Thank you for meeting me for the first time at DAV school. I cherish that first meeting fondly, and often go back to that moment in time in my imagination whenever you are away

and I miss you...

Thank you for holding my hand in the DAV school library with tearful eyes, and for letting me know that you would miss me a lot when I was away for a few days in Munger during Durga puja holiday...

4th

Thank you for sharing your DAV school

photographs and making me feel so special...

5th

Thank you so much for offering me delicious samosa and chutney from the DAV school's canteen. I truly relished them, and would like to eat them again with you when we visit Bokaro...

CHAPTER TWO

Long-distance love

Love was not easy for us, especially considering the long time we spent living apart from each other. After finishing my Year 12 at DAV school, Bokaro in 1994, I went to Aurangabad, Maharashtra to study hospitality at Taj's Hotel Management school.

Keeping in touch with each other through just phone and letters was not easy. As if this was not enough, I even had to leave India in 1998 to complete higher studies in Sydney, Australia.

Despite being continents apart from each other physically, our love continued to grow stronger through the fervour in our hearts. It was close to 10 years of a long-distance relationship from 1994 to 2004, which stood the test of time and you finally joined me in Australia in 2005 after our wedding in India.

6th

Thank you for giving me the most gigantic greeting card I had ever seen in my life, including numerous other greeting cards over the last 27 years, with heart touching messages expressing your true love for me...

7th

Thank you for spending all your money and time on international calls. It was so exciting to talk with you on the phone for hours when you were in India and I was in Australia....

8th

Thank you for holding my hand and making me feel cosy during cold winters in Chandigarh, Amritsar, Simla, Palampur, Mcleodganj, and Delhi when I visited you in India...

Thank you for those numerous trips to Hot Millions, Sagar Ratna and other restaurants in Chandigarh. I had a great time in Chandigarh and created many sweet memories with you...

10th

Thank you for roaming together in Amritsar, looking around for tandoori chicken and discovering "white tandoori chicken" for the first time, which was confusing due to its white appearance and different taste. In hindsight, it seemed a waste of time looking for tandoori chicken, but it was time well

spent together...

11th

I feel more confident in your presence. Knowing that you are with me helps me to solve life's challenges with greater sanity, objectivity and composure.

I thank you for your presence...

12th

Thank you for being so mindful, patient, and caring, when I get upset and may not be on my best behaviour. I love you very much for being my better half...

13th

Thank you for loving and visiting my family. I love you more every day for loving my family like your own. I thank God for allowing our paths to cross and for allowing me to love someone as incredible as you...

CHAPTER THREE

Welcome to Sydney

Your coming to Sydney in 2005 to join me was one of the happiest moments of my life. We finally managed to convince our parents to accept our relationship and to give their blessings to start our new life together in Australia.

Your joining me in Australia was an important milestone in my life. After you arrived here in Australia, life has been unfolding in a magical way, enabling us to live a fulfilled life. Your love, care and nurturing have played a significant role in helping me experience life more vividly with gratitude.

Mere realisation that you're my wife makes me feel blessed. Thanks a lot for uplifting my spirits with your smile, making every day a special day.

14th

You are the best thing that ever happened to me.
I am blessed to be with someone as beautiful,
generous, kind, and loving as you. I thank you for
all the wonderful things you have
done for me and the kids...

15th

I thank God for giving me a truly beautiful wife, both on the inside and outside. Thank you for choosing me as your life partner...

16th

Many thanks for looking after the family and preparing delicious meals and encouraging us to eat our meals together as a family...

17th

Thank you for looking after the plants and lawn

at home. Your magical touch

makes this home truly a sweet home...

18th

Thank you for playing Holi together at Darling Harbour with me and Keshish...

19th

Thank you for introducing me to your friends and family in Australia who are now very close to my heart...

Thank you for accepting my friends in Australia

as yours...

Life is more festive and enjoyable with friends and families...

Our friends and family members have positively
impacted our lives as they motivate and encourage
us to be a better version of ourselves...

Our friends have enriched our lives by enabling us to meet more kind souls and bright minds, thereby helping us to increase our circle of positivity...

Some of our friends are so close that we feel like they are part of our family. We are lucky to have such friends who can energise and inspire us to do things with greater love and awareness...

Our friends are a constant source of encouragement and inspiration. We thank our friends Pankaj and Anita for inspiring us to embark on a fascinating journey of doing karaoke and using music to open our heart to experience deeper love and connection...

Our family members have taught us to live in other people's hearts through smiles...

Returning to cultural roots through traditional dress....

We are so fortunate to have so many amazing

family members to share

our happiness with...

You became part of my family in a heartbeat
through your charming personality, for which I
will always be grateful to you...

All my family members love you for having such a
caring and loving personality...

You have won the hearts of all my family members through you genuine, loving and authentic nature...

20th

Thanks for going on the cruise holiday to the Sunshine coast together with the kids. I got to create many good memories during our time on the cruise together, especially the "Vodka Experience"...

Thanks for discovering the miraculous rock during the bushwalk which seemed to be infused wood and rock, reminding us of nature's effortless yet magnificent creations...

Thanks for having a passion for music and singing.

I enjoy listening to you when you sing...

23rd

Thanks for going to the "Hare Rama Hare Krishna" temple with the whole family. I enjoyed our time together watching nature unravel its beauty...

CHAPTER FOUR

Double bundle of joy

Our life together in Australia has been full of blessings. Between 2005 and 2015, we were fortunate enough to have two beautiful angels being born into our family, enabling us to become mum and dad.

I truly cherish countless loving memories of both Keshish and Karishma. The birth of our 1st daughter Keshish was a major milestone in our lives, allowing us to experience parenthood for the first time. I still remember how we named our first daughter by using the first half of our names Kesh+Ish which became "Keshish" which miraculously means "deep Attraction" in the Hindi language.

Our 2nd daughter was born in 2015, bringing even more happiness into our lives. Karishma's cheeky and bubbly nature makes me so happy.

24th

Thank you for bringing Keshish in this world and making me a father to such an adorable soul. Keshish's welcoming presence in our lives keeps bringing perennial joy and happiness, creating delightful memories filled with an everlasting state of gratitude and bliss...

25th

Thank you for bringing Karishma into this world too. Her bubbly and cheeky personality lights up our lives. Spending time with Karishma is truly a divine experience. Looking at
her beautiful face

when she drinks milk from the bottle feels so soothing and calming. This makes me admire the mystical power of nature and its angelic creations, invoking a deep sense of gratitude and love. Thank you for being a loving and nurturing mother to such a beautiful and divine child...

26th

Thank you for suggesting tutoring for Keshish. This has proven to be a life-changing decision for Keshish, resulting in quality education and career opportunities for her. This has only been possible due to your initiative...

Thank you for loving the kids so much and spoiling

them generously in a good way. Your love and

affection have aided Keshish and Karishma to grow

up being so confident

and independent...

28th

Thank you for allowing me to contribute to Keshish & Karishma growing together. This has been a delightful experience...

Thank you for encouraging me to go on holidays with the family. This has helped us as a family to create lots of beautiful memories worth cherishing forever...

30th

Thank you for motivating and guiding Keshish to become the bright, humble, curious, self-reliant and compassionate person that she is now...

31st

People do good deeds in their lives so they can go to heaven in the afterlife. I, however, experience heaven on earth daily due to your's and our kids' auspicious presence. Thanks for giving me this unique feeling of

"Heaven on Earth"...

Kids exist among us as God's reminder to love them unconditionally. Thank you for loving the kids unconditionally...

32nd

Thank you for encouraging Keshish and Karishma to sing and have a great time together enjoying music...

33rd

Thank you for taking Keshish and Karishma with us to the Royal National Park. The bushwalk rejuvenated us mentally, physically and spiritually...

34th

Thank you for going together to the amusement park with Karishma in Gosford. She had a great time there, making us feel very happy too...

35th

Thank you for helping me discover the joy of holidays with friends and family...

36th

Thank you so much for showering your love and affection on both kids. It's has been awesome to watch them both having a great time with you...

Thank you for giving me the pleasure of being a blessed father to two loving and talented kids...

38th

Thank you for bringing two adorable and curious kids into this world. I enjoy spending time with them very much. Interacting with them makes me feel happy and fulfilled...

Like Mother, like daughter...

Bundle of joy...

Keshish and Karishma enjoying sister time together...

love to see you all dressed up and

ready to rock and roll

and have a great time...

Karishma busy playing and learning...

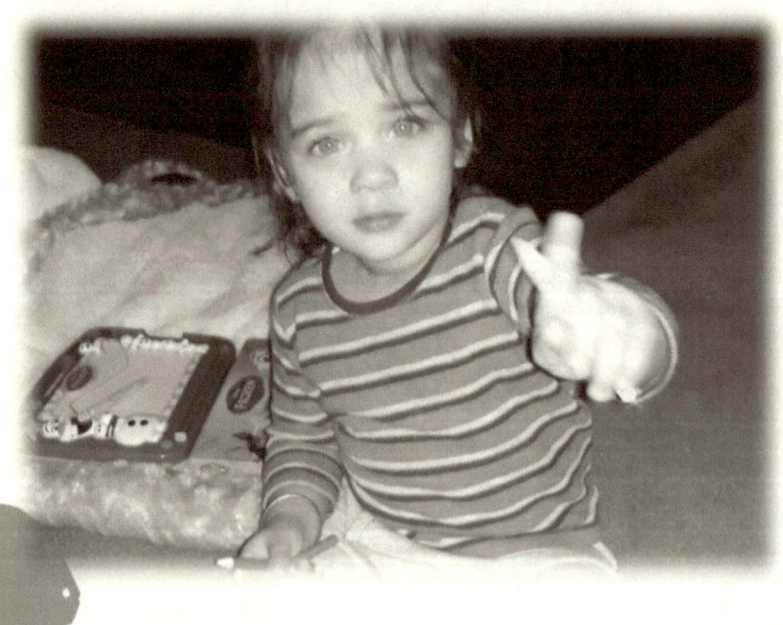

Karishma having "me time" with mum on the beach...

Keshish trying to learn and experience meditation for the first time...

Keshish having a great time with mum and grandmother...

Keshish and Karishma with maternal grandmother

and grandfather

exploring Sydney...

Karishma having outdoor fun with dad in the park...

Keshish having dad time...

Karishma spending precious moments with grandfather...

Keshish having grandfather time...

It great to see kids having

fun together...

Keshish doing art and craft session at Bunnings...

Keshish in holiday spirit...

CHAPTER FIVE

Gratitude

T rue love is evident and pervading in our lives by the grace of the Almighty. It has been nearly 27 years knowing each other and we have been on a long and adventurous journey together. We have experienced lots of miraculous moments and have created sweet memories. I am fortunate to experience life together with your loving presence and support. I am very grateful to you for all the big and small things you keep doing for me and the kids. I acknowledge your loving and caring attitude which is both praiseworthy and divine. I have realised that the highest emotion that we ever can aspire to is "love". In this chapter, I have also included my thanks and gratitude to family members in our lives who have contributed in various ways to help us create the life that we cherish now.

Cheating Death

On a hot summer afternoon in
November 2011, I was enjoying cool water
splashes with my daughter Keshish in the shallow
end of the community swimming pool.
I inadvertently ended up in the deep end of the
pool, panicked and ingested some water and ended
up lying unconscious and breathless
at the bottom of the pool.

Luckily Eric, an off-duty policer officer who was enjoying a family barbecue next to the pool, sensed danger, jumped over the fence, took me out of the pool, performed CPR and resuscitated me. My second daughter Karishma was born four years after the incident in the same month of November which seems like a miracle. I am deeply grateful to the Almighty and Eric for being able to give me a second chance at life and to have more opportunities to grow mentally, emotionally, and spiritually and experience life to its fullest. Thank you, Eric, for SAVING my life and giving me and my family a second chance...

39th

I feel truly blessed to have you as my wife and life partner. After having spent nearly 27 years together, I sincerely feel in my heart that you are the best wife and partner I could ever get in this life...

40th

I admire your beautiful eyes. They are truly mesmerizing and deep. They can look deep into my soul and fill me with love and joy...

41st

Thank you for being so supportive of my goals and being able to trust me to make decisions. You have created an impact on our family's present and future. It means a lot to me...

Like yin and yang, hot and cold, white and black,
we balance each other like the north and south
poles of a magnet. Thank you for being my equal
and opposite strength...

43rd

I am grateful to you for your affection attention,

support and care for me and other people around

us. Your presence has encouraged me to become a

better person.

I thank you dearly for that...

44th

Thank you for loving me and accepting me the way I am. Our relationship has helped me evolve socially, emotionally and spiritually...

45th

Thank you for joining me bushwalking in Leacock Regional Park. I had a good time drinking masala tea and chatting with you...

46th

Thank you for loving me the way you do. I thank God every day for giving me such a loving, caring, thoughtful, kind, and understanding wife like you. I would not be the husband and father that I am now without your love, support and compassion. ...

47th

Thank you for being such a charismatic, resilient, courageous, dedicated and wise life partner. Our years of living together have taught me many valuable life-lessons. You have helped me introspect, evaluate and understand myself better...

48th

Thank you for inviting me to eat vegetarian food for 40 days. This has helped me to become a vegetarian for life, resulting in enhanced physical and mental health...

49th

Thank you for possessing such a charming and captivating smile. God has blessed you with a great smile, so please continue smiling...

50th

Thanks for preparing and serving me more than 1000 cups of coffee and tea over 27 years of our journey through life together...

A special thanks to Jaswinder, the uncle with whom I have developed a special lifelong bond. Jaswinder's trust in my abilities and his inspiring and encouraging words have provided me with lots of inspiration. His wealth of knowledge as an entrepreneur, lecturer and a family man is commendable...

My mum's and dad's unconditional love towards me
has helped to become a better human being,
worthy of your love and companionship. Despite
hardships, my dad always gave me the freedom of
choice and resources that I deemed necessary to
excel. My parents taught me the value of simple
living and helping
others in need...

Thanks to your parents who were kind enough to put their trust in our decision to marry and blessed us to pursue our lives together. What a beautiful coincidence that your mum and I share the same birthday date! An even more pleasant coincidence is that your father and I believe in the power of yoga and meditation to stay healthy...

Your elder sister and her husband were your first family members who supported us. I am very grateful to them for their helpful attitude, reassurance and acceptance...

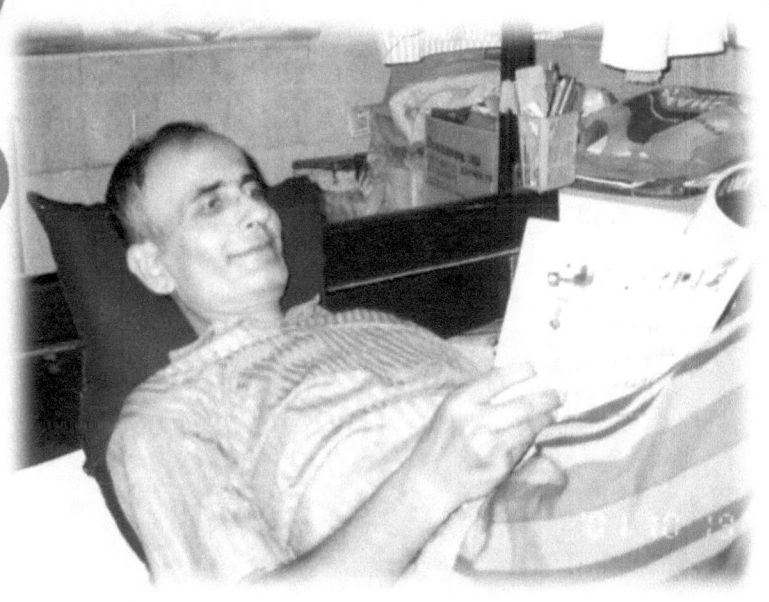

I am very grateful to my uncle for instilling and igniting within me the passion for reading books, which inspired me to embark on a life-long journey of acquiring knowledge and wisdom. It is due to his initiative that I was able to complete my education and set worthy life goals...

My grandfather would have loved to meet you. He sadly passed away long before I met you. I am sure his blessings will always be with us, despite him not being amongst us. I am so glad that my grandmother luckily had a chance to meet you. I want you to know that my grandmother loved you very much...

CHAPTER SIX

Sixteen principles of love

Through my journey of 27 years with my loving better half, I have learnt a few strategies or principles that seem to be working well in enhancing our relationship. I hope that sharing them with others may be of some help.

16 PRINCIPLES OF LOVE

Respect each other

Give pleasant surprises

Communicate honestly and authentically in a caring way

Spend "Us" time together frequently

Respect and accept your partner's family

Give space to each other

Do not keep scores

Address your partner's insecurities as soon as possible

Deal effectively with frustrations

Practice both internal and external forgiveness

Care for your partner

Resolve deeper conflicts as soon as possible

Express your love from your partner's perspective

Give your partner the benefit of the doubt

Accept and appreciate each other's differences

Celebrate together

1 - Respect each other

The word respect can mean different things to different people. A robust relationship must be built upon mutual respect. It's always good to discover what your partner expects you to do or say to show your respect towards each other.

Actions, behaviours and spoken words that may be normal and acceptable for one partner in a relationship may be hurtful and unacceptable to another partner. Knowing what is deemed respectful or disrespectful from your partner's perspective, and abiding by them, can contribute towards greater peace and love in a relationship.

Respect for your spouse should be mutual and reciprocal. Imagine how you feel when you sense disrespect in any shape or form from someone. Disrespectful acts or behaviour exhibited by our partner can potentially build up over time, and can be toxic and damaging in long run.

Valuing your partner's needs and feelings is of paramount importance. We must be respectful of each other's boundaries and be willing to listen and learn from our past experiences to improve relationships.

"ABOUT RESPECT"

1. Give the respect you hope to get from your partner proactively.
2. Respect each other's privacy because being in a relationship doesn't necessarily mean you have to share everything with your partner.
3. Respect can't be demanded; rather it has to be built mutually over time based on a foundation of genuine love and care for each other.

2 - Give pleasant surprises

One of the ways you can foster and grow your relationship is through pleasantly surprising your partner by expressing your love by giving surprise gifts, organising a surprise birthday or anniversary party for your partner, treating your better half to a shopping spree, giving flowers or breakfast in bed.

It could also be a vacation of your partner's choice to their favourite destination. Such surprises can potentially contribute toward fostering a closer and deeper relationship.

One of the basic human needs is to get a pleasant surprise in some or other form in our day to day lives. If you can occasionally give your partner a pleasant surprise, then you would be able to increase the level of excitement and thrill that can potentially contribute toward a more fulfilling relationship.

Knowing what your partner likes first and then choosing the right kind of surprise is important to avoid your well-meaning surprise turning into shock and stress for your partner and a disappointment for yourself!

Please remember that the surprise you intend to give should be something that your partner would like and genuinely enjoy and appreciate.

"SOME IDEAS TO SURPRISE YOUR PARTNER"

1. Create a romantic and soothing environment at home as a surprise for your partner after work.
2. Gift your partner their favourite concert ticket as a surprise.
3. Write a poem and recite it back to your partner.
4. Organise a surprise movie "binge night" and watch your favourite shows or movies with your partner.

3 - Communicate honestly and authentically in a caring way

C ommunication is the fulcrum of a healthy relationship. Honesty and authenticity in communication are very important as it allows both partners in a relationship to express their love as well as discuss any challenging issues. One very important element of effective communication is to refrain from any type of verbal or non-verbal hostility towards our partner.

Being patient enough for the right moment to discuss any challenging issue with our partner can be a good strategy. We all can fall prey to our raging emotional state and be unwilling to listen to our partner in the heat of the moment. Being caught up in an emotional rage, we may dismiss our partner's concerns as being frivolous and even lead to hurtful outbursts, damaging the relationship further.

No matter how challenging the issue may be, it must be communicated in a mutually caring way with genuine love and compassion for our partner.

"COMMUNICATION IS THE KEY"

1. Ask your partner open-ended questions and listen intently to learn more about your partner's needs, wants, and desires.
2. Encourage mutual discussion about issues which are upsetting either one or both partners in the relationship.
3. Listen to your partner with an open mind and be genuinely willing to offer support instead of criticism.
4. Be willing to change your own style of communication to make issues clearer, easier and non-offensive to your partner.

4 - Spend "Us" time together frequently

Partners need to spend time together frequently. Spending time together, giving each other our undivided attention without any distractions such as disrupting phone calls or messages, makes both partners feel loved and appreciated.

Depending on the common interests of both partners "Us" time could be as simple as watching a movie or having dinner together, bushwalking, hiking, cycling, visiting places of common interest or any other mutually agreeable activity. Please remember that both partners should be able to enjoy "Us" time activities otherwise they can lose their impact and significance.

"Us" time can help to rejuvenate the relationship, keeping the flame of love lit and passion alive in the relationship.

"IDEAS FOR DOING THINGS TOGETHER"

1. Take a class together to learn new skills such as singing, martial arts, cooking or any activity that you both enjoy and want to learn.

2. Teach your partner anything that he or she is interested in and you already know, like playing a musical instrument, pottery or painting.

3. Go together on a long drive with your partner occasionally, and do things together such as enjoying your favourite music, food or sharing pleasant memories.

5 - Respect and accept your partner's family

Our partner has family members in most cases. If we expect our partner to accept and respect our family members, then we need to have similar acceptance and respect for our partner's family members.

This can be quite challenging, but it is worth the effort.

We may think that our family members are special because they love us and have made sacrifices for our happiness and are there when we need them. Similarly, our partner has family members and our partner loves them. The sooner we make peace with our partner's family the easier it will be in the long run. Sometimes it may not be possible to accept our partner's specific family member due to major issues; in which case our partner should have empathy for us and respect our wishes.

Our partner has a past with his or her family members and acknowledging and accepting your partner's family members contributes towards harmonious co-existence.

Invite your partner's family occasionally to get together and do not deny their requests to join them for celebrating special occasions.

"SHOWING RESPECT AND ACCEPTANCE TOWARD'S YOUR PARTNER'S FAMILY"

1. Buy gifts for your partner's favourite family members.
2. Spend some time with your partner's family indoors or outdoors, and thank them for all their love and care.
3. Refrain from criticising any of your partner's family members or relatives, unless you have a genuine reason.

6 - Give space to each other

Giving space to our partner in our relationship is one of the ways that can assist our partner to refill their cup of energy and passion. "Me" time is equally important as "Us" time. Giving space in this context does not mean living apart from our partner under separate roofs but rather having mutual freedom to pursue our passions and hobbies that allows us to feel nourished and uplifted physically, mentally, emotionally and spiritually.

Spending some time away gives both partners the opportunity to miss each other. Giving space to each other can be great way to get some fresh air and reset ourselves emotionally, that can result in more healthy and desirable relationship. Striking the right balance is necessary for giving enough space and not drifting apart from each other..

Having occasional boys only or girls only outings or gatherings with our friends, pursuing our interests and hobbies without our partner, can help to break the monotony of daily routine.

"ME TIME HELPS TO REPLENISH AND NOURISH"

1. Dedicate 30 minutes after work daily to do something you want to do on your own, such as reading a book, journaling or pursuing activities that nourish us internally.

2. Proactively volunteer to look after kids and do household chores for few hours or a day to encourage your partner to pursue their own interests during this time. This can occasionally help your partner to relieve stress and feel recharged.

3. Go for an occasional solo expedition, such as fishing, golfing or go-karting to take your mind off regular chores and break the monotony.

7 - Do not keep scores

The habit of keeping scores can come naturally to most of us, and can be a very difficult thing to unlearn and overcome. However, keeping scores as to "who did what" can be very troubling and detrimental to a relationship, as it can diminish gratitude and fuel resentment.

One wise thing to do in a relationship is to appreciate every big or small thing done by your partner for you, which can encourage desirable behaviour.

As individuals, we only tend to see the tasks needing to be done for the home or a family member from our perspective, and overlook our partner's perspective. We need to see things from our partner's perspective and be appreciative of the fact that, if your partner does not take care of those things, who else will take care of them???

Reminding your partner how many things you do and how little he or she does can only lead to disagreement and bitterness which may build-up over time, damaging the relationship. We must expand our awareness as a couple to appreciate the contributions of our partner and try to see each situation from their viewpoint and be empathic.

"AVOID KEEPING SCORES"

1. Marriage is more of a co-habitation than a competition.
2. Avoid getting tangled in any type of competitive tendencies that may lead to harbouring negative emotions such as envy, rage, annoyance, disgust or sadness.
3. Discourage yourself from the urge to outsmart or outwit your partner during conversations, and explaining how you are better or more important than your partner.

8 - Address your partner's insecurities as soon as possible

We all feel insecure and vulnerable for a variety of reasons from time to time. It must be a high priority for both partners to address any insecurities they have about their partner, no matter how small they may appear.

Ignoring signs of any insecurity brewing within your partner's mind can be detrimental to the relationship. Not dealing with your partner's insecurities can lead to extremely challenging situations later when the troubling issue that is "just the size of a mole ends up growing into a mountain", making it more difficult to resolve. Any psychological damage stemming from insecurities can be sometimes irreversible, so should not be taken lightly.

Being observant and proactive in dealing with any types of securities, whether emotional, physical or financial, is vital for a healthy relationship.

We must be the first one to proactively take the initiative to support and assure our partner, so they can overcome their insecurities.

Overthinking your partner's attitude and behaviour can, at times, lead to insecurities arising due to mental fear and uncertainty, and therefore needs to be managed effectively by becoming rational and pragmatic.

"STOP THE MOLE FROM TURNING INTO A MOUNTAIN"

1. Human beings can get emotionally charged up over small and futile issues, therefore we need to take charge of our emotions and how we respond to a situation at hand.

2. Self-esteem building activities such as exercising, sports, self-care and other activities that you are passionate about can help to reduce or eliminate emotional insecurities to a certain extent.

3. We should trust our partner and our instincts about any situation to uncover the issues behind our insecurities and work towards eradicating them.

9 - Deal effectively with frustrations

Having frustrations in a relationship can range from being just mildly irritating to extreme frustrations capable causing serious problems such as mental illness, depression and even separation or divorce. Frustrations should be dealt with as quickly as possible to minimize the collateral damage to the relationship.

Each partner in the relationship perceives frustrations differently and we, as unique individuals with a different set of values, need to deal with our frustrations effectively.

Lack of communication is one of the most common reasons for frustration for a couple. Other things that can contribute towards frustrations in a relationship are our partner's different values, lack of intimacy, uncaring attitude, money-related issues, infidelity, excessive expectations from each other, and relying on our partner's validation to feel happy and content.

Any threatening situation that causes frustration must be dealt with by seeking professional help, such as counselling or therapy.

Doing different things such as meditation, yoga or any form of physical exercise, playing or listening to musical instruments, painting, engaging in any interesting art or craft can help to relax and unwind and assist in reducing frustrations.

Some ways to reduce or eliminate frustrations could include talking to someone trustworthy to take the pressure off our chest and also making necessary changes to minimise situations and circumstances leading to frustration.

Accepting things that you cannot change and actively changing things that you can will help to reduce or eliminate frustrations.

"EFFECTIVE WAYS TO DEAL WITH FRUSTRATIONS"

1. Be willing to change your communication style to make it non-ambiguous, easier and non-offensive to your partner.

2. Frustrations can at times stem from stress at work or home. Finding positive ways to vent stress can be very beneficial for mental and emotional wellbeing.

3. Doing some physical activities such as running, weightlifting, boxing, or any type of physical sports can be effective in reducing stress.

10 - Care for your partner

Caring for your loved one is very important. The amount of effort needed to keep the relationship boat sailing happily is often underestimated by both partners. Nurturing and caring for your partner is the core foundation of long-lasting love. By living together and observing our partner, it is possible to learn and do the things that make our partner feel loved and cared for.

Caring can be expressed in multiple ways. Any act of kindness, a bouquet of flowers, written or spoken words of appreciation, helping with shopping or household work, genuinely listening to our partner's issues or saying the magic words "I love you" while looking into your partner's eyes can all be construed as different ways to express our love and care.

Trying to do what our partner considers caring should be the preferred way of caring for our partner.

For some, receiving flowers means a lot while, for others, genuine compliments or spending time together, or just being able to listen to our partner, can make them feel loved and cared for.

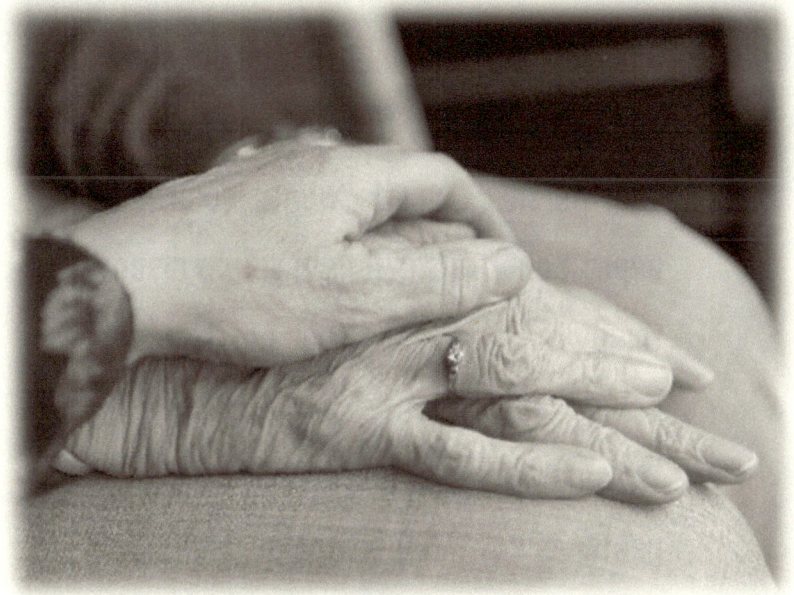

We must refrain from reprimanding our partner in front of others, as it can lead to resentment.

Listen to your partner with an open mind when he or she is talking and be genuinely willing to offer support instead of criticism.

"CARING FOR OUR LOVED ONE"

1. Ask your partner open-ended questions and listen intently to learn more about your partner's needs, wants, desires and aspirations. This can help you to discover things that can make your partner feel being taken care of.

2. We must strive to learn what caring gestures our partner prefers and be willing to bestow them, as and when required.

3. Be aware that your way of feeling being cared for could be different from your partner's way of feeling being cared for.

11 - Practice both internal and external forgiveness

Making mistake is an inherent part of human nature. Any relationship, therefore, requires both partners to have the ability to forgive their loved one for the relationship to thrive. Unarguably, forgiving and letting go is easier said than done.

We all have a hard time forgiving, therefore be assured you are not alone in struggling to forgive.

The ability to forgive and let go of past hurts is one of the most effective strategies we can deploy to strengthen and fortify our relationship. Harbouring and fuelling grudges due to hurtful events can take a toll on our mental and emotional wellbeing. According to a study at Johns Hopkins University, an act of forgiveness can reduce the risk of cardiovascular disease, lower blood pressure, anxiety, stress and depression.

Forgiving your partner externally may appear to be fine from our partner's perspective but, from your standpoint, it is the internal forgiveness that is true forgiveness because it frees us from negative emotions, and thus reduce the chances of an emotional outburst later.

Holding grudges has been shown to contribute towards mental and physical illness over a prolonged duration. Forgiveness is not just an emotional process but has positive health benefits too.

Let go of past hurts and optimize your mental, emotional and physical healing.

"FORGIVENESS LEADS TO INNER PEACE"

1. Not being able to forgive in extreme situations, such as when being subjected to violence and abuse is normal. In such cases, forgiveness can be an internal process, being mindful of the fact that forgiving is something you are doing for your wellbeing.

2. Forgiving our partner for a perceived or implied hurtful act does not mean that we must remain in the relationship with them, especially if any type of violent behaviour is involved that creates safety or security concerns.

3. Meditative techniques, such as the Sedona, Ho'oponopono and Silva methods, may help to take a more methodical and structured approach towards the forgiving process,

12 - Resolve deeper conflicts as soon as possible

Most couples have conflicts due to varied reasons, and therefore it is very important to be vigilant for any warning signs of potential conflict. The love between a couple can easily fall back into the "law of familiarity" zone over years of living together, and run out of the passion. Partners may start to perceive those behaviours and activities in their partner that were acceptable and desirable earlier appear to be annoying, irritating and even downright unacceptable.

If little conflicts are left unattended due to ignorance or denial, these trivial conflicts may grow tentacles and become mammoth and deep later. Engaging proactively to resolve and diffuse small conflicts on a regular basis as they arise can be helpful in avoiding long term conflicts of a deeper nature.

This deterioration phase in a relationship can be very strenuous on both partners, and can lead to the sowing of seeds of conflict over an extended period. In rare circumstances, when both partners hold a drastically different set of values, goals and vision, they could end up being at a crossroads in life that need deeper soul-searching.

If you or your partner is physically or mentally tired, getting some rest before you start talking can be a helpful strategy. Being in a rested state can make us more rational and empathic. Offering choices, giving hope and being appreciative of our partner's contribution to the family and household can also lead to diffusing the tension between both partners.

Do not respond when you are in a state of anger, as this may result in reciprocal anger and do more damage than resolve and de-escalate the situation.

"SOME HELPFUL IDEAS FOR MITIGATING AND RESOLVING CONFLICTS"

1. Refrain from getting too close physically when talking to your partner, especially when you are in a helpless state of anger, rage or fury, and be respectful of your partner's personal space.

2. There may be some issues for which commonly agreed resolution may be difficult to reach, due to a partner having different values and life experiences. When caught between "a rock and a hard place", we need to exercise profound wisdom by being able to peacefully and respectfully "agree to disagree", and be willing to cohabit and flourish despite differences in our values and life experiences.

13 - Express your love from your partner's perspective

Learning our partner's love language can help us discover ways to make them feel appreciated and loved. "Us" time can help both partners to unwind and reconnect on a deeper level. Brainstorming several "Us" time activities and choosing the most exciting one that both partners genuinely enjoy is crucial for bonding and feeling loved.

We feel emotionally exhausted occasionally and may start to fall short of commitment towards the relationship. When encountering such a situation, recalling all our partner's appreciative attributes can refill our hearts with appreciation and gratitude and elevate us emotionally. Being human makes us naturally susceptible to emotional rollercoasters, however we must choose to act and exhibit positive behaviour towards our partner in such challenging moments.

Being aware of our partner's likes and dislikes and refraining from pushing each other's buttons can help to maintain peace, and potentially increase our love and affection for one another.

Look into your partner's eyes and offer a cuddle and express your love and appreciation verbally, or the way she or he wants it.

"STRATEGIES FOR EXPRESSING LOVE"

1. Give your partner the gift she or he has been longing for.
2. Offer to do household chores or fix something that has been waiting for ages to be fixed.
3. Present your partner with a gift card or voucher to splurge on themselves occasionally.
4. Periodically do things for your partner with unconditional love and compassion, without expecting anything in return.

14 - Give your partner the benefit of the doubt

Relationships are built on the foundation of trust between two people, who must be willing to look out for each other for the rest of their lives. There will be situations faced by couples in a relationship that may create doubts in partner's mind, and risk the relationship being adversely impacted, or even result in separation.

Trust, at times, can be even more important than love, as it can boost the relationship or take it downhill when trust is diminished or breached due to either partner's action.

Giving the benefit of the doubt to our partner does not mean that one or the other partner is weak or more dependent on the other.

Trust is the core fuel that powers the relationship, and we must do all it takes to earn the trust of our partner. Long distance relationships can work only when trust is intact. Doubts destroy relationships.

It simply means that we, as humans, can easily fall prey to negative emotional states and do things that we would not contemplate doing when in a stable emotional state.

When faced with doubtful circumstances involving our partner, we should be willing to give the benefit of the doubt to our partner and practise compassion and forgiveness, even when we think that our partner has wronged us.

"WHAT TO DO WHEN YOU FEEL DOUBTFUL ABOUT YOUR PARTNER"

1. One technique to use when faced with a situation where you need to give the benefit of the doubt to your partner is to ask yourself would what just has happened matter after 10 years or not.

2. Doubts can sabotage a relationship and push away the person you love long before you even realise the root cause of the mistrust or doubt.

3. Do not talk about your doubts to people who can turn your doubts into real issues and worsen the situation, based on their biased views. They may hold secret grudges or even have ulterior motives to deflect you in some way.

15 - Accept and appreciate each other's differences

Being accepted and appreciated is one of the essential human needs and, when used effectively, can help a relationship to thrive. Partners generally have complementary qualities and values, but sometimes can be opposing. This is a perfectly normal situation we should expect to face when we enter any relationship.

The key to a thriving and lasting relationship is to accept our partner's complementary values and qualities.

We must accept how unique and different our partner is and learn to enjoy the differences. By accepting and appreciating unique qualities of our partners, we raise their self-esteem and enhance trust, thereby contributing positively towards the relationship.

The family and household need different things and, depending on your partner's values and qualities, they can take the lead and complete work that they are more passionate about.

Ask your partner periodically if their needs are being met, and is there anything that you can do to help.

"SOME WAYS TO EXPRESS ACCEPTANCE AND APPRECIATION "

1. Write a love letter to your partner, expressing your love authentically by recalling special moments you have shared together.

2. Share your personal experiences with your partner if they show genuine interest. Sharing personal experiences can potentially forge a deeper connection and bonding over time and develops understanding from each other's perspective.

3. Another very effective way to express appreciation towards your partner is to publicly acknowledge what your partner does for you and express your gratitude to him or her.

16 - Celebrate together

Celebrating birthdays, anniversaries and events of social, family or religious significance together can create opportunities for couples to do things together and potentially provide opportunities to strengthen the bond between couples.

They can be a reminder of life's journey being about "Us" rather than about individual achievements and pursuits. Common interests

such as dancing, singing and reading can also become a reason to celebrate together.

Life is precious in different ways. We must strive to praise its beauty and mystic nature and be grateful. The more we acknowledge, appreciate and celebrate our life, the more reasons we will eventually discover to celebrate".

"SOME OCCASIONS TO CELEBRATE"

1. Birthdays of family members, turning 16, 18 21, 30, 40, 50, 60 and so on.

2. Milestone marriage anniversaries, such as 5th, 10th, 25th, 50th, 75th and so on.

3. Our partner or kids' graduation from school or college, or getting their first job or promotion.

4. Family members receiving any kind of public recognition in the form of awards or any other type of acknowledgement.

5. Your partner, yourself or any other family member getting new job or promotion.

6. Buying a new house, car or any other item of significant emotional value for you, your partner or any family member.

CHAPTER SEVEN

Journal for practising the principles of love

A journaling section has been included to write down your own authentic and brilliant actionable ideas that can assist in enhancing your relationship with your spouse or a life partner.

Each of the 16 principles of love has a dedicated section to write down actionable ideas or strategies that come naturally to you and are aligned with your values. These ideas could be acted upon later to elevate your relationship leading it to a better, deeper and fulfilling relationship on the emotional, physical and mental level.

Printable copy of the journal can be downloaded absolutely freely (no need to register) from
https://tinyurl.com/relationshipjournal

Love Principle 1

Respect each other

Please write down 5 or more actionable ideas or strategies that you feel can help you in this area.

_____

_____

_____

_____

_____

_____

_____

_____

_____

_____

Love Principle 2

Give pleasant surprises

Please write down 5 or more actionable ideas or strategies that you feel can help you in this area.

_____

_____

_____

_____

_____

_____

_____

_____

_____

_____

_____

_____

Love Principle 3

Communicate honestly and authentically in a caring way

Please write down 5 or more actionable ideas or strategies that you feel can help you in this area.

_____

_____

_____

_____

_____

_____

_____

_____

_____

_____

Love Principle 4

Spend "Us" time together frequently

Please write down 5 or more actionable ideas or strategies that you feel can help you in this area.

_____

_____

_____

_____

_____

_____

_____

_____

_____

_____

_____

Love Principle 5

Respect and accept your partner's family

Please write down 5 or more actionable ideas or strategies that you feel can help you in this area.

_____

_____

_____

_____

_____

_____

_____

_____

_____

_____

_____

Love Principle 6

Give space to each other

Please write down 5 or more actionable ideas or strategies that you feel can help you in this area.

_____

_____

_____

_____

_____

_____

_____

_____

_____

_____

_____

_____

_____

Love Principle 7

Do not keep scores

Please write down 5 or more actionable ideas or strategies that you feel can help you in this area.

_____

_____

_____

_____

_____

_____

_____

_____

_____

_____

_____

Love Principle 8

Address your partner's insecurities as soon as possible

Please write down 5 or more actionable ideas or strategies that you feel can help you in this area.

_____

_____

_____

_____

_____

_____

_____

_____

_____

_____

_____

Love Principle 9

Deal effectively with frustrations

Please write down 5 or more actionable ideas or strategies that you feel can help you in this area.

_____

_____

_____

_____

_____

_____

_____

_____

_____

_____

Love Principle 10

Care for your partner

Please write down 5 or more actionable ideas or strategies that you feel can help you in this area.

_____

_____

_____

_____

_____

_____

_____

_____

_____

_____

_____

Love Principle 11

Practice both internal and external forgiveness

Please write down 5 or more actionable ideas or strategies that you feel can help you in this area.

_____

_____

_____

_____

_____

_____

_____

_____

_____

_____

Love Principle 12

Resolve deeper conflicts as soon as possible

Please write down 5 or more actionable ideas or strategies that you feel can help you in this area.

_____

_____

_____

_____

_____

_____

_____

_____

_____

_____

_____

Love Principle 13

Express your love from your partner's perspective

Please write down 5 or more actionable ideas or strategies that you feel can help you in this area.

_____

_____

_____

_____

_____

_____

_____

_____

_____

_____

Love Principle 14

Give your partner the benefit of the doubt

Please write down 5 or more actionable ideas or strategies that you feel can help you in this area.

_____

_____

_____

_____

_____

_____

_____

_____

_____

_____

_____

Love Principle 15

Accept and appreciate each other's differences

Please write down 5 or more actionable ideas or strategies that you feel can help you in this area.

_____

_____

_____

_____

_____

_____

_____

_____

_____

_____

Love Principle 16

Celebrate together

Please write down 5 or more actionable ideas or strategies that you feel can help you in this area.

_____

_____

_____

_____

_____

_____

_____

_____

_____

_____

_____

_____

Thank you for marrying me…

FREE APP OFFER FOR DEVELOPING POSITIVE MINDSET

Download the App for  Android smartphone/tablet at

https://tinyurl.com/affirmationapp

This affirmation app has inbuilt brainwaves sound and white noise which can be used for developing positive mindset and can help you to stay focused and achieve your goals. The brainwaves synchronization has been found to enhance relaxation response and positive influence cognitive abilities. There are six categories of affirmations included - happiness, health, success, wealth, relationship and weight loss. Each of these categories have 15 affirmations which can be further edited to give it more personal touch for improved effectiveness. You can even add more categories and affirmations or edit or delete the existing ones to have unique user experience and customization.

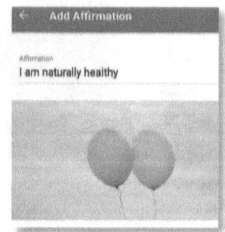

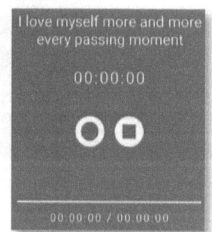

This App is compatible ONLY with Android smartphones and tablets.
This App is NOT COMPATIBLE with iOS (Apple) smartphones and tablets.

Dear Ishpreet,

Thank you once again for spending 27 precious

years of your life with me and many more years

to come...Love you from bottom of my heart...

Yours Forever,

Keshav...

In the end, all that will be left to

ponder upon are...

Whom We Loved

Who Loved Us

And

Did We Love Enough...

-- Quote by Keshav Jha

MORE BOOKS BY KESHAV JHA

Visit

www.maxlifepublishing.com

HOW TO MAKE BETTER DECISONS

Develop Effective Thinking & Decision Making Skills

KESHAV JHA

BEING

Become Happy in
as Little as
30 Seconds NOW

HAPPY

200
PROVEN EASY & QUICK WAYS
TO BECOME MORE HAPPY

KESHAV JHA

Sureshot Ways to Achieve Goals

3 Steps Goal Setting For Teenageers

KESHAV JHA

POWERFUL & EFFECTIVE
"Me Time"
STRATEGIES

HOW TO
FILL YOUR
OWN
CUP

200
SELF-LOVE IDEAS
"Learn to Love Yourself"

KESHAV JHA

STOP PROCRASTINATION

100 SMART STRATEGIES FOR OVERCOMING PROCRASTINATION

KESHAV JHA

USE THE POWER OF
YOUR SUBCONSCIOUS
MIND

SUBCONSCIOUS
MIND
MASTERY
EASY AND PROVEN WAYS TO
PROGRAM YOURSELF FOR
EXTRAORDINARY
SUCCESS

KESHAV JHA

YOGA
For
BETTER LIVING

CREATE
HIGH ENERGY
LIFE !
DEVELOP HEALTHY MIND AND BODY

KESHAV JHA

ANCIENT WISDOM
for
ENGLIGHTENED LIVING

YOGA VASISTHA

Simplified

KESHAV JHA

"Lots of people want to ride with you in the limo. But you want someone who'll help you catch the bus."

— Oprah Winfrey

"The central idea of love is not even a relationship commitment, the first thing is a personal commitment to be the best version of yourself with or without that person that you're with. You have to every single day — mind, body, and spirit — wake up with a commitment to be better."

— Will Smith

"Where there is love, there is life."

— Mahatma Gandhi

"The beginning of love is to let those we love be perfectly themselves, and not to twist them to fit our own image. Otherwise, we love only the reflection of ourselves we find it them."

— Thomas Merton